Soul sculpting

BY
S. SUGANTHI

COPYRIGHTS

Copyrights@2022, S.Suganthi

ACKNOWLEDGEMENT

First of all, I would love to express our gratitude to the almighty and publication house for giving this opportunity. I thank everyone for their huge effort in the completion of this book.

The contents are made sure to be free of plagiarism.

ABOUT THE BOOK

"Soul Sculpting" is written by S. Suganthi. This book is full of soulfull poems which are the phrases from profound heart of author.

AUTHOR

S.SUGANTHI

S. Suganthi, a budding writer who has been writing for over two years. She provides philosophical writings. Her educational background in English literature has given her a broad base for writings. Writing is her hobby, habit, passion and love. Between reality and fantasy, she writes her thoughts. Her books are available in Amazon Kindle named Heartly Sayings and Healing journey-1.

CONTENTS

YOU'RE MORE WORTHY

Last night, I talked to the stars
About the mishaps of the universe
And the hustles prevailing everywhere.
I blew out the haste in my town,
What echoes in my ears nowadays
Are the city noises
That constantly reminds me
The need to fasten up my pace,
Else I might stay behind
While the time moves ahead.

Concealed in the sheets of self-doubt,
It's been too long
Since I've been running away
To fit myself among the places
That don't echo about my existence.
This world has raised us
In an imaginary world of perfection,
Laying down the terms and conditions
Full of abstract myopic beliefs.

The stars told me
To let the rhymes of reality
Thread their way into my mind,
Regardless of
What they fill up my ears with.
They wanted me to know
That I need not to mold myself
In the shape of their toxic standards,

Rather fly to the surroundings
Where my heart doesn't feel bounded
And know how to inhale the tranquility of freedom.

The melancholic weaving of stars
Made my eyes see the haste of the universe,
Sometimes, even the sun too
Tried to fit among the night stars
But, the darkness outshined the light of the sun,
For it wasn't meant to be there.
While the day opened up his arms
And let the sun form a home
Amid the brightness of dawn,
For it knows that the sun
Is worth more than the dark.

The world has always been like this,
Filled with people
Who would never see your worth,
And those who knows you're worth something.
It now depends on us,
Whom we pay attention to.

*****

BREAK THE CAGE OF COMPARISONS

She scribbles her dreams
On the crumbled pieces of
Paper with the ink of misogyny,
Licks them with the salty tears
And dump into the plastic jar
Created by the enemies
Of her growth
Who envy the steps
She has built for herself,
A disastrous storm prevails
Beneath her ribcage,
An unknown voice screams there
Struggling hard to be heard
But the noises of heartbreaks
Can be beaten by those of judgements.
She is just another victim
Of the patriarchy.

He pats himself
Under the moonlight,
The sun has set
And so are the voices of his heart.
Smashed beneath the responsibilities,
His lungs now longs
To breathe a little more freely,
While he isn't supposed to cry
For the tears might seem
As a weakness
To someone who
Doesn't care about his strengths.

He is just another victim
Of toxic masculinity.

Remember the twelve year old you
Who always longed to grow up
And do more than cherishing
The aspirations you had,
If they are now narrowed down
Under the laid standards of society,
Or have succumbed
Beneath the layers of insecurities,
How would you ever respond back
To the little kid in you
Who had shine in his eyes.
To soar as high as bird,
You need to learn
To flutter the wings
As fearlessly as birds.
Break the cage of comparisons,
And learn to fly irrespective of
How far is the destination.

*****

FAILURES ARE AN ILLUSION

Life is a mixture of
The little moments
That smashed inside
Breaking the doors of positivity,
Crumbling the flowers of hope,
And other moments
Bringing sunshine to the garden,
Raindrops singing an ode
For the plants to regrow,
What makes the aura beautiful
Is the way you perceive things.

This isn't to tell you
To always look at the bright side,
But to tell you
That no matter how dark it gets
The light would never fail
To illuminate a little part of your life.

Something about this generation
Narrows down my heart
And dry the wings of my soul,
The barren lands of patience
We've grown up with
Certainly made us look ourselves
As nothing but disappointments.
The reflection we see in mirrors
After minor accidents we face,
Or a few broken expectations
That we find hard to inhale,

It screams loud enough
To shatter our hearts,
But we forget to question ourselves,
Was it really the end?

If the new beginnings lie ahead,
Certainly it was just a phase
And not the whole dream
That died in a matter of days.
Failure, is perhaps nothing,
But an illusion we come across,
Only to be tested by the universe,
The passion we have
To walk over the path of challenges.

*****

BEWARE OF LOVE

The universe in my mind is bigger than what
You've portrayed at your side,
On a starry night
You told me
The love you've confined,
A part of me bounced
While another narrowed down.

You fell for the image
You've built in your head
While the truth somewhere remains uncared,
I am not only what you've seen rather a thousand worlds
in me rotate underneath.

Invade my thoughts
And you would see countless riots, there are more to my
fantasies and the dreams I've adorned. Rushing through
the parts of me, some wild, others being sensitive, tell
me, if you would stay
Even if I lag behind in this race, this race of perfection.

Tuck me around your waist,
Hold me tighter
In your heart amid all the haste. Darling, there are parts
of me that are little strange,
I've lived a thousand stories
Some real, others just in my head, a few are still running

there, you're unaware of my harshest storms, you won't
drown, I promise,
Yet I may not always shine,
Unlike those fairies.

INDIVISIBLE CHAIN

The stars visited my world yesterday where my toes
shivers with cold
Which I served them unknowingly,
Now they are scared to tap once again,
What if the land glides under my feet
And my stale body forgets to rise again.

This world now seems so scary
Everything I've done here, eventually
Had slid me into the bowl of sorrows,
Smiles I used to adorn over my face
Have now rushed into corners
And had hid themselves in unknown places.

The raindrops on my stained window settled as the
messages from the sky singing a melody of harsh
adversities of life, we are here for uncertain but limited
time.

The locked doors of my head
Feels like the rooms I've chosen to be enclosed in, the
demons in there haunt me daily,
It feels like I've tied myself with indivisible chains, and
now the bird in me is tired
Of fluttering her wings,
For it hasn't been able to fly since long.

Perhaps, the worst phases in life
Come with the battles of heart and mind, they don't hold
swords and armor
But rips apart one's flesh deeper
Than those little war equipments,
One such happens while deciding
If you should hold on or let go.
Even if every part of you
Screams to grab their arms,
And bolt them inside your almera,
Yet sometimes you've to choose the departure, for it
would only wilt those flowers
Amid the suffocated quarters,
Only to outspread the foul smell,
And harm you later.

*****

SHINE EVERYDAY

This is to those who are stuck amid the dusty walls
Shedding the grey tears out of the melancholy, i know
the flowers of hope
That you used to nourish
With your love and care
Have now wilted
And are deprived of all the nutrients
Which they need to thrive again.
This isn't tell you to stop mourning over them, but to
remind you
That they aren't dead yet,
And you've to accumulate the strength
To water the roots
And let those flowers once again bloom.

I've been there too,
When your head spins reciting billion thoughts, even
your blues seem colourless,
And everything around wreaks havoc. Dip your brushes
of pain
In the metaphors of inspiring poetries and paint your
own scars
With the colours of patience and faith. Cry if you want
to,
Scream loud enough to silence
The voices inside for a while,
But, don't let the calm inside
Be destroyed by the chaos outside.

Crying never tells you're weak
Rather denotes the strength you hold. Even the ocean
faces storms and waves, but there is nothing harsh
enough
To deteriorate the calm it holds.
Let your heart become the home
To the peace that your soul deserves.
Life will have frequent waves,
But those who know to stay serene,
Will pass through them
And thrive fiercely till the end.
To grow, you need to rise from the ashes, even the stars
have to collapse before shining.

*****

I WISH

If there exists a parallel universe, i wish the stars there
Never fall to shine as a hope
In the eyes of aimless strangers,
The sky never looks down
To measure the distance with the ground,
The lovers never seperate
And the strength never deteriorates.

If there exists a parallel universe,
I wish the weeds never grow
Amid the garden of dandelions, every petal of rose flexes
its beauty without the harshness of flowers.

If there exists a parallel universe,
I wish the bones never shiver in dread
And the darkness isn't considered bad.
The blues aren't destined to be a metaphor to the sorrows
and distress,
While the hearts never pierces itself
With the overflowing buckets of thoughts.

If there exists a parallel universe,
I wish the bumps of life
Never trios a human down,
But then i wonder,
How would humans ever learn to rise?

If there exists a parallel universe,
I hope the life never changes its colours, but then,
How would one ever paint their sky

With the rainbow hues?
The rain alone is never sufficient
To have the rainbow framed.

FORGET THE MISHAPS

Yesterday, I heard someone mourning over the battles
between heart and mind,
I couldn't stop thinking about
How the rebellion in me has settled quiet nowadays, too
tired to fight with itself,
They say it's worst, when there is
Disagreement between your heart and mind,
But, how do we forget to talk about
The forbidden fate of those
Whose hearts don't speak any more.

The sourness of my dreams
Have wilted the flowers of my hopes, these pale walls
now echo
The times I didn't listen to the naive heart, and now it is
least bothered
About sparkling my eyes with happiness.

My days are made up of the thoughts
That i want to grab tightly
And carve them out of my brain,
The sensation that arises
Whenever a past memory flashes in front of me, i wish i
could twist them all together
And throw them somewhere far.

I look around
And for me it's tough to find the eyes that carries no pain
And the throats that haven't swallowed the syrups of
melancholy every day.

My friend told me
To forget the mishaps and move on,
Only if I could,
I would forget that the flowers are meant to die, the stars
are fated with the darkness,
The ocean can never reach the sky,
The clouds can never hug the grounds.

I'm tired,
Not of these heartbreaks
But from running in a hope to heal.
The more I try to escape,
The faster this reality chases me.

Now I recite the mantra of acceptance, for nothing else
can ever cure the wounds.

*****

UNPREDICTABLE LIFE

Brings unexpected storms but unexpected sunshine too,
stay for the latter to arrive

Drown in my eyes,
You would see the suffocation floating on the uneven
surface of battles, anything i see nowadays
Doesn't feel like a home to me.
Did you too cry last night?
I wonder how many strangers accompany me from the
distance,
In flowing and wiping off the tears every time i dump
my ache on the bed, the only way for the loners
To lighten the weight of their heart.

I wish to pour out to someone
My wants to laugh out loud
While all that comes out are the silent screams, enclosed
in the masks of smiles.
Everything nowadays seems to be slipping away, would
I ever come back to the times
When did i felt okay?

The worst thing about
Always pretending to be happy is,
At the end of the day
When you look into the mirror,
Your own reflection starts questioning you. Your inner
self gets stuck amid the voices asking "why have you
been smiling
When you don't want to?

Whom are you fooling,
Them or yourself?"

What I keep telling my heart is,
If every day can't be a good day
Then every day can't be a bad one either.
I try hard to not lose my hope amid the blues. After all, if
life gives unexpected storms,
Then it may give unexpected sunshine too.

*****

ECHOES OF PEOPLE

My ears ring with the echoes of the people running in
haste,
Everyone around moves back and forth,
Half of them daydreams
Lost in their own thoughts,
Carrying silence on the lips fluently,
Other half suppressing the heaviness
With the bulky words.
Will this loop of rush ever end?

My mirror often screams the ugliness iam tired of
carrying all around, insecurities crawl nastily in my
veins only to turn my blood blue,
The coldness wrapping me in its arm while the sun isn't
bright enough
To melt this ache with its warmth.

Someone once asked me,
If the sky holds my peaceful breaths or the ocean waves
calm my soul, I am still searching for the answer
wondering why one has to be ditched for the other one to
be chosen?

This city is full of neglected dreams
In a quest of being superior,
Goofy brains roaming all around seeking success among
myopic beliefs, while the key to happiness
Has been locked by themselves
In the cage of comparisons.

*****

BOLD ENOUGH

Is it just a tear drop falling
From my eyelashes on my palm
Or the screams of my tired soul
That I have confined since so long?
Forgive me for letting my emotions
Flow from the valleys of heartbreaks,
But the ocean inside now feels overburdened,
This flood within is now too heavy
For me to carry.

I would smile for you
As and when you say,
Suppressing all my sorrows
Under the little happiness i've got.
But, some days the volcano in me
Bursts the fire out,
For the suffocation inside choke my lungs
And now they long to inhale freely.

My mother injects power in me
Wiping off my tears,
Claiming i am bold enough
To net let these adversities drown me.
But, even the happiest flowers

Are destined to wilt someday,
Even the toughest person
Melts sometime.

GOD SEES EVERYTHING

We all have been fed with a lie
About being good and bad,
But, if we see there is nothing
As right or wrong, but just a perspective.
Good and bad as morals
Aren't nouns, but adjectives,
Yet we are too ignorant
That we weld them to human hearts.

The walls of temple nearby
Confine the longings of devotees
And the complaints full of melancholy.
The words carved on them echoe
"god sees everything,"
What if he doesn't?
What if he does,
And yet ignores the offenses
As we humans do.

I say, god may for once, let you go,
But your own soul
Would for sure become the slave
To the piled up guilts inside your heart
At the end,
The sins you've committed
Won't bother anyone but you.
The mirror will remind you

Of the hardships you've put others into,
The city noises will ring
The cries of innocents in your ears,
It would all pierce your own self,
For one can run away
From anyone but themself.

LIFE IS WEIRD

Life is weird, humans are more.
We see about hundred people a day,
Some we notice, some we don't.

Most of them are having hearts
Heavier than the grey clouds in the sky
Some want to rain, some don't.
But, what bothers me more is
That the faces
Which are smiling the most,
Have the stories of weeping behind.
They've lived in the moments
Which are now just confined to their hearts.
They've shed the tears
Thinking they would probably never end,
And some are
Still crying somewhere inside
Yet are moving without any pause in life.

This is the generation of broken hearts
Running away from the pain
As they think it's the only way to heal.
But,
How do you expect this pain to end,
When you don't let it begin.
People want to see the light
At the end of the tunnel,
But, what's wrong is,
They don' strive
To move ahead to reach the end.

The universe often echoes these verses,
To let the light enter your heart,
You should be willing to leave the dark.

*****

REALITY

Concealed in the sheets of self-doubt,
It's been too long
Since you're running away
To fit yourself among the places
That don't echo about your existence.
It isn't about blaming you,
But this world has raised us
In an imaginary world of perfection,
Laying down the terms and conditions
Full of abstract myopic beliefs.

Let the rhymes of reality
Thread their way into your mind,
Regardless of what the world
Has filled up your ears with.
I want you to know
That you need not to mold yourself
In their toxic standards,
Rather fly to the surroundings
Where your heart doesn't feel bounded
And knows how to inhale
The tranqulity of freedom.

Even if the verses of your music
Don't go along with their odes,
That in any way,
Doesn't let down your grace.
My heart has nothing but the unpleasant
Antiques of my memory
That often reminds me of how

I tried to frame the hoax of my emotions,
In order to be accepted by them,
Only to stuck later in this loophole.

Push your brain cells to question yourself,
"would you still be the same,
If the society hasn't told you
How you're supposed to be?"
Maybe you would prefer
The sand of beaches to find solace in,
And not the silence of mountains
To dream about.
Maybe you would paint
Your sky with black and white,
If they haven't told you
That colours are all
What you should chase.

You can choose to be a lily,
Even if the whole galaxy
Start to admire the beauty of roses.
You can prefer to dance in the rain,
Even if those clouds scream
About the soothness of sunlight.
You have every right
To adore the moon,
When they are busy
Romanticising the stars.

Strive to shine better
As you already are,
Rather than trying to become
What you are not.

MIXED EMOTIONS

What I feel nowadays
Is nothing more than twisted emotions
Crawling inside my happiness
Only to tear it all apart
The loneliness that reside within
Soaks the particles of joy,
Only to make me gulp down my pain
And spill it out later
With my only companion, poetry.

Everyone around too
Are more or less the same,
Strangers I meet have their eyes
Dancing on the rhymes of poetry,
Dipped into the hardships,
They all move back and forth
Carrying the baggage of problems.
Each of them have similar,
Yet different ache.

The thing about poetry is,
It rushes into your soul,
Light up the soothness
In the places that are tired of dark,
You would drown into it
But the streams would make you rise.

Purest form of love to exist is poetry,
You would lose yourself in it
Without having a single minute of regret,
Even after knowing
That you're not the only one
Falling for it,
Neither it only loves you.

Every heart beats poetry
Some just know how to carve it out
In the form of words
With the ink of metaphors.

*****

CHAOS OF LIFE

Mouths filled with judgements,
I've seen strangers chewing
Their absurd beliefs about others,
Only to conclude their personalities
Based on a few thoughts they've.

The sorrows run down my neck
Along the seas of bitter truths,
Everyone around are blindfolded
With the layers of assumptions,
They've built a home of myopia
Only to limit their own perceptions.

I asked my mother,
Why she sits in the corner
Turning television on and off
Again and again,
In the little time she gets for herself,
Even though she has dreams
That are waiting to be fulfilled,
Her silent broad smile
With the pain in her eyes
Speaks all about the criticism
That would be welcomed
With her move to chase the dreams.

The breeze yesterday whispered in my ears,
How humans are blessed enough
To share their hearts out,
I told her, how we don't have

The audacity to adorn our blessings,
Rather have mastered the art
Of turning our fate unfortunate,
By not allowing anyone
To open up without making them feel
That they would be judged.

Hardly, anyone knows
What we've been through,
And the least we can do
Amid the chaos of lives,
Is allowing others to become
What they wish to be.

HEARTACHE FLOWS

Some people won't ever
Understand the hollowness
Stimulating in your heart
When your loud screams
Often go unheard amid crowds,
Being surrounded by
Known strangers
Yet having nothing
But loneliness
Thriving within.
And I understand that,
So does my poetry.

Heartache flows down my chin,
The shivers have formed
Their permanent residence here,
The situation of feeling nothing
Yet feeling too much
At the same time
Dangles on my wide opened jaw,
Slowly I am trying
To gulp it all down
But my stomach is too sensitive
That it often chokes
Within its intestines,
Having indigestion with my pain.

Everyone around complains
About the changes prevailing
And growing in me,

No one ever tried to dive into
The sorrows that made me
What I never was.

Half of my days are
Made up of the self-doubts
Growing on my bones,
The stem of love is now incomplete
And I hope for you
To grow flowers on it.
All I ask from others
Is to invade in my life
Only if they plan to stay.
Stay, not only when
I will be the same
But even if,
A part of me begins to change.
Love me like you love the moon,
For darling, I won't always be full.

*****

MOCKING JUDGEMENTS

Wind often hides
Behind my curtain to tell me
The stories of hopeless strangers,
Who trips on the thresholds
Due to the hustling thoughts
Which have occupied their brain cells,
And their eyes have lost
The nerves to let them remind of hindrances.

What breaks my heart nowadays
Aren't the teary eyes of my friends,
Rather the fractured heart
They've been carrying since long
Under the veil of widest smiles.

The bird on my window pane
Asked me why humans
Confine their feelings to themselves
When they're privileged enough to speak
I told her we've enough words
But not the ears
That would appreciate our emotions.
Some listen to us to let the rain fll
And make our grey hearts lighter,
Others listen to us
To throw their mocking judgements.

The gloomy flowers on the isolated bridge
Were enunciating the lost lovers' trauma,
They've been forming a home

Near the dried lands,
This world has been too harsh
To show them the benevolence
They've been starving for.

Lately, I've realised I don't hate people
Rather the series of questions
Followed by their hatred comments
That push me towards self-doubt.

We all are so busy in echoing our sorrows,
That the pain in other person's eyes
Become invisible to our naive heart
Perhaps, we haven't encountered
Someone who would show us kindness,
But, what makes us less of a human
Are the places we could be kind
And be the reason behind someone's smile,
But we chose to not.
Maybe, we could be that someone.
It takes strength
To be kind amid the loopholes of unkindness.

*****

LOST LOVERS

Everyone tells you
There is always a light
At the end of the tunnel,
But no one ever justified
Why the tunnel
Is wrapped in the darkness.

Here it is for the lost lovers,
The dizziness you're stinging with
In a hope for the nourishment
From that special someone,
It is only here
For the taps of self-love to open up
That you've fixed in your heart,
This won't dry you
Rather, let you know
How to water your own roots.

Here it is for the bewildered youth,
I know the doors seem locked
Right in front of you,
While you're conflicting with the inner self,
On which one to open up,
The keys are lost
And the screws are tightened,
This is all muddling up your threads,
But this chaos is here
To let you know
The place peace deserves in your life.

Here it is for the crushed hearts,
It takes sadness,
To enjoy the spoonful of happiness.
We humans are weird,
Complaining is our standard
While gratitude is lost somewhere.

If it wasn't for the rain,
We would never appreciate the sun.
These phases of darkness
Will teach you
The importance of light in life.

*****

BROKEN STARS

When you flip the pages of your destiny
And look behind to the broken stars
That have already fallen apart,
You become the salt and pepper
To your own wounds,
Only to make them deeper.

With every step you put forward,
It will hurt a little lesser.
And with your every turn to the past,
It will only unfold the sheets of pain.
You can't change what has happened,
And save yourself from being injured,
All you can do is to use the ointment to heal,
And to stop touching your wounds
For they are only going to hurt.

It's not easy to get out of such phases
Somedays you'll feel like
You're drowning in the pain
Of your own mistakes,
And there is no one to pull you out.
Other days, you'll find your home
In the ocean of suffering you're stuck in.

I won't say that you'll heal abruptly,
Neither I will tell you that it's magical.
But, you have to allow yourself
To find the support that will save you.

Let it hurt, let it ache.
But don't let it bleed forever,
Don't conclude that this is the end.
There are numerous blank pages
That you need to fill with your own creations,
Pages which don't hold the stories of your damage,
Pages which don't have the ink of your sorrows,
And to fill the empty pages of future with happiness,
You have to stop turning back to the old pages of grief.

*****

HOPES

Remember the eve
You cheered to the sky
With the dreams
You've been weaving,
A part of you gathered the strength
To raise the bars of expectations
And visualise
What ten years from now
Your life would look like,
While the other part
That was supposed to drag
You to that threshold
Remained silent, staring at the sky,
Waiting for the breeze
To fly you to your dream destination.

The sixteen year old me,
Who never knew to cherish life
Learnt the art of admiring
The little drops of rain
Forming pearls over petals,
When saw the bigger griefs diving in,
The worst part of growing up is
Life doesn't become easier
As the four year old us
Thought it to be,
Rather each stage carries
A different and harsher test,
While somehow our souls
Forget to find life in little moments.

The more I talk
To the seconds that passed away
The more I realise
It was never the time
That had put one's aspirations
On the flame of failures,
Rather the lack of yearnings
Or more specifically,
The shortcomings in efforts
Which apparently burnt most dreams.
For each minute you wasted
To blame it ll on destiny,
Somewhere, someone, practiced
A little more than you,
Success isn't just hungry for longings
Rather for the endeavors.
Go high on efforts
And not just on hopes.

PARENTS

Just letting you all know
How lucky you are, if you
Have parents who support
You when you are down
Mentally, you are lucky
When there is no comparison
Game in your home, when
Your relatives have very
Less chance to point their
Fingers at you. Understand,
Not everyone have their
Parents as good as yours,
Appreciate if you are not
One among those children
Or people who wait to
Have a good conversation with
Their parents, appreciate your
Life if your parents won't
Order you do things, appreciate
Your life if you don't
Have to explain, don't feel
Like moving out from your
Home, appreciate your life
If you have never asked
God why you are burden
To your parents, appreciate
For everything that comes
To you without asking, there
Are parents who treat their
Children as just the trash even how

Good they are, how much hard
They work on their life to make
Their parents proud. There are
People who always want
Their parents to be happy but
They see something's always
Wrong in whatever they do,
Remember you'll not everyone's
Life is as good as yours.
Appreciate your life having
Things that are not easy
For so many out there.

*****

BE KIND

People hurt people, because
Everyone are opinionated,
Everyone will have their
Own mood swings, everyone
Who supports us also tend
To hurt us sometime or the
Other by knowingly or
Unknowingly. A company that
Always makes us smile and
Changes our mood is important.
Having someone or only one
Who never or hurts
Very very less number of
Times is important for
Our mental health.
Companion that never hurts
For being whatever we are,
Companion that shows love
By without expecting
Anything in return,
Companion that makes
Us smile and laugh when
We are not able to is more
Important. Not hurting
Is important, caring for
The one who cares for is

Important, prioritising
Who needs to be is Important.

*****

ACCEPT EVERYTHING

I don't know how
One can easily take
Others granted,
Most importantly
One that shows
Good care
Towards and one
That shares
Good bond with you.
Accepting everything
They said and everything
You've been in is just
Fake has another
Level of gut one
Must have.
Everyone these days
Should understand
That relationships with
People are important,
Bonding with them,
Time you share and
Spend is important
Not just socialising
For one own benefit
Isn't, cheating on friends,
Taking granted and
Never apologising
Always had me at
The surprise of shock.
While running into the

World of excellence,
With everything
Moving to be a better,
I see one part of the
World loosing
Humanity, trust,
Loyalty, bonds and
They undoubtedly
Taken a leap atFailing.

*****

I HAVE HEARD

I have heard that the tears are nothing more than
emotions
And nothing less than the pain
That never found the metaphors
And alphabets enough to fit in.
They often peek through
The curtains of eyelashes,
To see if the one standing in front
Would care enough to wipe them
Or just laugh out loud over the sufferings.

I have also heard about the sunsets,
That the sun drown itself
Somewhere amid the clouds at night,
For giving boundless space
To the other stars to reflect their shine,
Oh, the love like this isn't everyone's cup of tea. But, the
fact is
The sun neither sets nor rises,
Perhaps, even the most selfless love
Is nothing but an illusion nowadays.

I saw someone yesterday
Having no reason to believe in "everything happens for a
reason" and no energy left to "trust the process." I saw
someone else too yesterday, having faith in the universe
Even after having no reason to. Some people are living,
Some are only waiting for death,
I hope, you're the former one.
The thing is

No one waits for the sunlight
If it is not after the storm.
It takes us difficulties
To pat the luxuries we have got.

LONG-DISTANCE LOVE

All I have you is at miles and miles distance away,
With no fragrance of love,
With no affection in all the shallow space in my heart.
Things which are far lock beautiful,
We are apart may
Because we are meant to be beautiful being apart,
Maybe we are meant to be the ocean and sky.
You wrench my heart even miles apart,
Your soul attracts me even sitting oceans away,
No matter how much so ever the distance we have
between us,
We are just like the sky and earth,
Who seem beautiful if they meet,
But they aren't meant to meet.
We are like the sun and rainbow who meet only when
there is a rain between us.
You are beautiful to me staying far away.

*****

BROKEN LOVE

Cause it isn't easy for me to accept this life not having
you,
It rips my heart to think of the days i cannot have you in
there,
I can lend anything to have you for this life
But can't lend this heart and still not have you,
My tears would have made an ocean if i could store
every time
They weep thinking about you,
My colourful days became so blue,
I could've grown a garden if I plant them every time
I think of you, the life i see around seem dumb just like
the nature before the heavy rain,
I close my eyes to see the memories to cherish,
I realise I don't have any even.
I inhale your thoughts and exhale the poetry day by day,
they take down all the pain my heart carrying over the
years,
I hope you stay happy wherever you are,
I have you in my heart
No matter how far you are anyway,
That way I will repair my lost smile and reappear happy.

*****

MOONLIGHT

I am is just another day,
Another day with full of light and waiting for the moon
to arrive,
For the shine it brings into my life.
My heart weighs a lot carrying mountains of pain in the
name of you,
Every inch of it says only your name.
Every piece of it bleeds seeking you as if it cut through
the shards of glass.
My feelings said you are almost mine,
Which never took the name of love.
What did I do?
 to have this life full of just hopes with no reasons,
What did I wish for?
For the misery that i can't handle?
My heart screams that it wait for you as long as the wind
passes, as long as the tides run,
As long as i have you in my heart.
I wait for the moon with love,
I wait for my heart to fix herself,
I wait for the love to have home,
I wait for the days, that shine brightly as beautiful as a
Moon light has.

*****

LIVE OFFLINE LIFE

This world seem perfect while
You look through anything from far.
It actually is not the same as what you see.
How and what you are at home at present sitting and
scrolling this, that's how everyone in reality.
Don't stress yourself to be that so called people on
internet.
Who inspires you on internet,
They inspire you to be the better you,
But you don't have to be them in your life.
You don't know how many tears they are holding behind
their lashes,
Behind their cameras,
Yet they are strong.
You don't know how much they are going through
Yet they come back stronger be it stress, depressed and
anxiety they are dealing with.
Sitting there, just comparing and making yourself less
Than any others will not benefit you to earn anything.
Believe in yourself for what you are,
Know what you are good at,
Learn how to make your interests as a secondary source
of income if it can't be primary,
Accept to have a new habit daily,
A healthy comparison will always bring good from you
while the unhealthy one will make you even worse than
what you are,
Choose what you want to. Be you for your better you.

*****

GUITAR - MOON

Guitar doesn't know,
From where those musical sounds are,
But the one who plays does.
Moon doesn't know,
The sparkling shine it has,
But the sun who sets does.
So does, you never know t
He sparkles you have,
The strength you hold,
The victory you make,
The happiness you give,
But this world who made you this way does.

*****

DEPARTURE

The fact that everything has an end
Bothers me as much as it pleases me.
The song that takes me back to him,
I hope it could never wave a goodbye,
Just like he did.
But then,
How would i ever find a song,
That will take me back to myself
The way his departure did.

Every struggle is after all
Followed by the beautiful things
That we have never imagined,
Just like the sky
Is followed by the sunshine
After every harsh rainfall.

They call me crazy
To be this obsessed with the sky,
I call them unfortunate
For they could never cherish
The beauty that up there lies.
The clouds paint the sky grey often,
When they can't hold the rain any longer.
But the sky never mourns,
Rather let the clouds shower,
Singing an ode of bravery.

Wind rushes through my ears,
Whispering the melody
To tell me how I will rise up stronger,
Just like the sky do,
Turning pink after its blues.
The greys of the sky tell me,
How courageous one should be,
The sky turning pink tells me,
How resilient one must be.

*****

HEART V/S MIND

On some days my heart is
The cigar rolled in lost lover's hand,
That is soon going to end
After reducing the ache
Of the broken heart,
But burdening my own self
With the weights of self harm.
Mind says stop hurting yourself
For those who don't even care,
Who are just going to blame you
In the words they later share.
While this naive heart
Abide by its goodness and purity
Believing that to heal others
Is too its duty.

On some days my heart is
The broken leg of vintage chair
Dwelling in the grandma's room,
Being used and thrown
And tagged as nothing
But fruitless seeds being sown.
Least do anyone realise
How i've been carrying
The heaviness of others' heart
For making their soul comfortable.
Mind says go ahead
Leaving everything behind,
But the heart echoes its decency,
"what if they need you another time?"

On some days my heart is
The incomplete book
Covered with dust in the shelf
Of uneasy and timid writer,
Which craves to be completed.
Mind says, collect all you're left with
And run to the one
Who'll rejoin you to make you complete.
Heart fights back once again
With the sword of its generosity,
Asking what if i leave
And they lose their sanity?

*****

BILLION THOUGHTS

My head is a home to a billion
Thoughts
Scratching the corners of my brain cells,
And my heart endures the pain
Of leaving you behind to move on.
Nothing hurts more than knowing
That the one you've thought to be real
Was nothing but an illusion.

My heart is made up
Of the petals of wilted flower
Emitting the foul smell of heartbreaks,
Longing to be rejoined again
And float in the garden of serenity.

My nights are nothing
But a trail of thoughts with teary eyes
And tired mind,
Hurting my own heart
With the memories you left behind.

My thoughts are graveyard
To the vessels of love filled with void,
Eating up a part of me everyday
Recalling the moments
When you were unloving me.

My words are nothing
But the alphabets
Dipped in the buckets of metaphors

Forming the traces of pain
That i wish to vent out,
To silence the chaos inside
With the blood spilling out in poetry

My expectations are nothing
But the sword piercing all my dreams,
Letting my hope flow in the valleys
To dry the roots i have been trying to nourish.
Yet, I am learning to let go of the things,
Which prevents me from blooming.

*****

YOU OWE THIS TO YOURSELF

The worst feelings in the world are
Composed of
The mishaps and ruined expectations,
When the thing we wanted the most,
Turns out to be the exact opposite
Than what we have always pictured in our minds.

Being a kid, we all wanted to be an adult,
Or maybe not,
We just wanted to be wiser and independent,
Which is actually
Accompanied by countless struggles.
As we grew up,
We realised that this independence is scary.
What seemed to be light weighted,
Actually comes with the heaviest burdens.
While adulthood gives us
The competencies to make our own decisions,
We are often stuck in a maze
That our own mind has formed.
It is a liberty
Which won't ever set you free.

What are we nowadays,
If not the prisoners of maybes and what-ifs,
Enclosed in the envelopes of sometimes,
Scared and hopeful at the same time.

Who is our own, if not ourselves?
We've all fallen for someone
Who was never there to pick us up.
Lost in the big arcades of our heart,
Sliding in our own rivers of emotions,
We reached to the dried shore
With the wilted and bruised petals
Only to end up all alone.

What is life,
If not the meadow of lessons
Trying to grow us every day,
In a way that will never be known.
Love harder each day,
But sprinkle the colours of love
On your own art foremost.
Do everything in love,
But don't rip yourself apart for someone,
Who would never try to rejoin you.
You owe this to yourself

*****

CHAINS OF FATE

Sometimes I wonder,
What if we pull ourselves back
From forming a home inside people,
Who some or the other day
Are destined to leave,
Some by choice,
Others by binding themselves
In the chains of fate.

It feels like every part of your body
Being ripped apart
With the sword of realities,
When your favourite person
Whom you thought to be yours forever,
Slips away in no time.
Not only the luxuries being snatched,
But your soul starts feeling homeless.

But, what if we don't build our homes
Inside people rather in our dreams.
The one thing i have learnt from life is,
The more you chase people,
The farther you slip away
From your dreams.
There are some people
Who would make you feel closer
To your dreams,
But even they fade away someday,
Leaving you in a chaotic state.
You'll end up in despair once again,

For forever isn't meant for people
But the imprints they leave
On our heart and mind.

Perhaps, we will grow fiercer
If we try to make dreams
Our permanent companion,
Rather than seeking people
To hold our hands.
Mayhap, we would never be homeless
If we make our dreams, our first home.
For people to leave, dreams don't.

*****

I AM NOTHING BUT

I am nothing but
A small part of the big world,
And the biggest part of my small world.
Nothing more than a small grain
In the sack of billions,
And nothing less than everything
That my own soul needs.

I am nothing but the splits
That unwanted setbacks of life have left,
Every part of my body
Echoes the shivers of blurred history,
Calling out for the ointments
To tape the cracks that are still burning.

I am nothing but the jumble
Of unheard emotions and unsaid feelings,
Floating among the poisoned tears,
Forbidding the widest smiles,
For now my cheeks ache out of the
Words that I never spoke in dread.

I am nothing but the grey clouds
Overwhelming myself
With the burdens of unfallen rain,
Due to the thought that no one
Would be there to hold me in arms,
In case i fall.

I am nothing but a wilted flower,
Waiting to be nourished by the gardeners,
Least did I realise that on some days,
We need to nurture our own roots
To grow like dandelions
And bloom like sunflowers.

I am nothing now, but a muse
To my own dried and barren lands,
For now I've chosen to seal all the
Leaking rivers of blood in my heart
With the bandage of self-love.
How naive I was to seek the light all around,
When I carry the whole sun within me
You don't need anyone else to heal.

*****

DON'T SCARED OF RAIN

Some days,
I let my bottled up insecurities
Echo the silence, grieving over
What could have happened,
If the things never took the turn
Towards unfavorable circumstances.

We humans are made up of the
Abandoned happiness in lively heart
And meticulous sorrows buried inside.
About sixty percent of human body
Is nothing but the water,
Mine has turned all of them into tears.

I wish I had realised this sooner
That the situations and struggles
Don't hurt us as much as we ourselves do,
The tendency to think that
"all this could have been better"
Leaves us in a pitiful state of mind.
How negligent we all are
To ignore the fact
"it could have been worse"
Winding up all our strength in mourning.

Hope is a dreadful thing
For those who aren't prepared for the storm,
Not always the light is
As nearer as it seems to be.
But you should always have enough strength,

To walk in the dark till the end.
Just because you should hope for
Better days,
It never means,
To leave the courage packed
In the blanket of positivity,
Rather you should wear it daily.
Hope for the sunshine,
But don't be scared of the rain.

*****

SHATTERED HOPES

Wobbling lands of my thoughts
Have entangled the strings in my head,
The battles of my mind
Between the crumbled dreams
And the shattered hopes
Sometimes make the air around me suffocated.

The faded walls of my room
Echo the restless voices of heartbreaks,
Confined in those boundaries
Are the times
I cried to myself loudly in inaudible screams,
Times when my favourite dresses didn't fit
And the curves of my body became a curse,
Times when the dark circles
Over my face became the center of conversations
Amid the group of judgements,
Times when my bedsheet gathered
The dusty complaints of my naive heart,
Times when nothing seemed right,
Those walls provided me the warmth
When everyone around turned heartless.

When I was a kid,
I often thought to myself
That the adults never hurt them
For they are sensible enough
To move ahead without tripping.
Least did I know
That they're actually sensible enough

To hide their injuries behind the smiles.
We grow wiser each day.
But never become the wisest.
Perhaps, that"s why life seems so cruel.

Sometimes I wonder
That out of the thousand people we see daily,
Is there anyone
Who hadn't been through such roughness.
Perhaps, no.
Yet, we all tend to keep moving,
What can be stronger than that?

*****

THANK YOU FOR READING